Positive Living

This book, *Positive Living Through Positive Affirmations* is written with you in mind. Every affirmation is designed to empower you each DAY as you embark on your spiritual, personal, and professional journey. Let's face it, life can be difficult at times and because of its complexity, it's easy to get off course and distracted. That's why I wrote this book – to keep you focused and to make sure you're headed in the right direction.

There are 365 affirmations. Each DAY, I encourage you to read it and meditate on it. You will find that each affirmation will speak to you and your situation. The great thing about this book is that everyone (no matter how old you are) can read it. That's right, all faiths, cultures, and ethnicities will be able to gain something positive from this book. Everyone needs positive affirmation.

Through my years of writing, I felt the call to publish this book to help out my fellow brothers and sisters who need encouragement. I don't care about your educational degrees, political affiliation, or social status because if the truth is allowed to be told, all of us need to hear and read something positive.

About the Author:

An inspirational speaker, motivator, author, organizer and "liberator of persons from all intellectual, social and cultural walks of life", Dr. Sinclair Grey, III is a committed advocate for communal change. As a strong proponent of gathering the masses through grassroots efforts, Dr. Grey has dedicated much of his life to mobilizing and inspiring others to achieve their true potential.

A native of the Washington, DC metropolitan area, Dr. Grey graduated with a Bachelor of Arts degree in Criminology from the University of Maryland, College Park, Maryland, in 1991. After receiving his call to preach in 1997, Dr. Grey earned a Master's of Divinity degree and graduated Cum Laude from the Samuel DeWitt Proctor School of Theology at Virginia Union University, Richmond, Virginia, in 2002. He is a certified NTU Psychotherapist and has received certificates of completion from The Addiction Prevention and Recovery Administration in psychopharmacology and adolescent and addiction issues in addition to serving as a facilitator for a Rites of Passage program geared toward young males. He also conducted voter registration drives in Virginia and Washington, DC; participated in a protest march against police brutality in Philadelphia, Pennsylvania, and spearheaded an Anti-Prostitution protest in Washington, DC; organized a conference on Domestic Violence Against Women and appeared as a guest speaker in various forums including the National Black Religious Summit on Sexuality and the DC Department of Family Preservation Teen Assessment Program. In 2012, Dr. Grey was awarded a doctorate of divinity degree from St. Thomas Christian University in Jacksonville, Florida.

Acknowledging his ability to relate to young people, Dr. Grey served as a Project Director with Progressive Life Center in Washington, DC, where he oversaw a mentoring program geared toward children whose parents were incarcerated. He has made appearances on radio talk shows including Interfaith Radio. Reverend Grey is also the author of three books, ***Seeds of Freedom: Inspirational Messages for Ordinary People with Extraordinary Potential, God Held Back Your Night So That You Can Get It Right***, and ***It's In You: Motivational Messages That Will Help Uplift and Empower You.***

Dr. Grey was inducted into Cambridge's Who's Who for his work in advocating empowerment and justice within the church and country as a whole.

Dr. Grey currently writes daily inspirational messages that travel throughout the world. His daily inspirational messages is currently heard on Montgomery Alabama's station, Hallelujah 104.3fm and read in The Soul Pitt Quarterly Magazine in Pittsburgh, Pa. In addition to this, Dr. Grey has spoken to various audiences such as insurance companies, telecommunication firms, and nursing homes, just to name a few. Without a doubt, Dr. Grey loves what he does and wants to empower as many people as possible.

To contact Dr. Sinclair Grey III, call 301.699.8904 or email: drgrey@sinclairgrey.org

DAY 1

Inconsistency leads to insufficiency.

Thoughts:

_____
_____
_____
_____
_____
_____
_____

DAY 2

If you want a blessing, you have to first be a blessing.

Thoughts:

_____
_____
_____
_____
_____
_____
_____

DAY 3

Cheer yourself up everyday. The more you encourage yourself, the better you'll feel about yourself.

Thoughts:

_____
_____
_____
_____
_____
_____
_____

DAY 4

Dreams die when you give up and give in.

Thoughts:

_____
_____
_____
_____
_____
_____
_____

DAY 5

Failure to maximize effort will result in failure to receive blessings.

Thoughts:
_____
_____
_____
_____
_____
_____
_____

DAY 6

The more joy you have on the inside, the less you worry about the weather on the outside. In other words, true inner joy radiates no matter what happens.

Thoughts:

_____
_____
_____
_____
_____
_____
_____

DAY 7

A person who refuses to listen to wisdom and act on its advice is a person who refuses to leave the plantation of stupidity.

Thoughts:
_____
_____
_____
_____
_____
_____
_____

DAY 8

Dialogue that is meaningful and productive will create solutions that are impactful.

Thoughts:
_____
_____
_____
_____
_____
_____
_____

DAY 9

Education should never force you to deal with the status quo. In a real sense, education should cause you to create opportunities for freedom.

Thoughts:
_____
_____
_____
_____
_____
_____
_____
_____

DAY 10

Reading books that are designed to challenge you elevates your consciousness and intellect. Books that make you question, analyze, and critique helps the mind remain sharp.

Thoughts:

_____
_____
_____
_____
_____
_____
_____

DAY 11

Whether you do good or bad, you'll always have people who'll hate on you. Here's my advice. It's more important what you do for God that matters. God allows haters to make you stronger and sends you blessed people to open doors for you.

Thoughts:

_____
_____
_____
_____
_____
_____
_____

DAY 12

The moment you settle for settling is the moment you throw away what God has for you.

Thoughts:
_____
_____
_____
_____
_____
_____
_____

DAY 13

Every moment contemplating on what isn't going right keeps you away from thinking and doing what is right.

Thoughts:
_____
_____
_____
_____
_____
_____
_____

DAY 14

Fear is the gravitational force that hinders your ability to soar.

Thoughts:

_____
_____
_____
_____
_____
_____
_____

DAY 15

Through God's unconditional love and mercy for you, He's able to restore and resurrect your life when unpredictable things occur.

Thoughts:
_____
_____
_____
_____
_____
_____
_____

DAY 16

If you want to reach a high altitude, you must first change your attitude.

Thoughts:

_____
_____
_____
_____
_____
_____
_____

DAY 17

Today is different from yesterday. It can be the beginning of something new while yesterday is a memory. Here's your shout – Today is filled with promise and potential.

Thoughts:

_____
_____
_____
_____
_____
_____
_____

DAY 18

No matter how many degrees a person has, learning must never end.

Thoughts:

_____
_____
_____
_____
_____
_____
_____

DAY 19

Don't let where you are in your reality define what God has for you in your destiny.

Thoughts:
_____
_____
_____
_____
_____
_____
_____

DAY 20

You can't step out on faith if you allow fear to order your steps.

Thoughts:
_____
_____
_____
_____
_____
_____
_____

DAY 21

With God and through God, your today and your tomorrow can be better than your yesterday.

Thoughts:
_____
_____
_____
_____
_____
_____
_____

DAY 22

Stay positive in your thoughts.

Thoughts:

_____
_____
_____
_____
_____
_____
_____

DAY 23

A person without vision is similar to a person in quicksand – going nowhere but down.

Thoughts:

_____
_____
_____
_____
_____
_____
_____

DAY 24

Those who don't support your goals and dreams don't need to be in your circle. Simply put - associate with those who are positive and helpful.

Thoughts:

_____
_____
_____
_____
_____
_____
_____

DAY 25

You can't expect the best out of others if you're not willing to put out the best of yourself.

Thoughts:

_____
_____
_____
_____
_____
_____
_____

DAY 26

Happiness is such a rarity that once you find it, you have to work to maintain it.

Thoughts:
___
___
___
___
___
___
___
___

DAY 27

With God first in your life, all things are possible.

Thoughts:

_____
_____
_____
_____
_____
_____
_____

DAY 28

Forgiveness is the catalyst to healing. In addition, forgiveness allows the love of God to cover you from head to toe.

Thoughts:

_____
_____
_____
_____
_____
_____
_____

DAY 29

Today is filled with hope and possibilities. Grab on to it and walk in victory knowing that you can do all things through Christ who strengthens you.

Thoughts:

_____
_____
_____
_____
_____
_____
_____

DAY 30

Live your life to please God not for the validation or approval of others.

Thoughts:

_____
_____
_____
_____
_____
_____
_____

DAY 31

All of us make mistakes and will make mistakes. However, it's the person who repents and asks for God's forgiveness that God will renew and restore.

Thoughts:
_____
_____
_____
_____
_____
_____

DAY 32

Through our imperfections, we have the One and True Living God who is able to sustain us, redeem us, redirect us, and continually love us. Always remember, God loves you and only wants the best for you.

Thoughts:

_____
_____
_____
_____
_____
_____
_____

DAY 33

No matter what life throws at you, never lose your faith in God.

Thoughts:

_____
_____
_____
_____
_____
_____
_____

DAY 34

Never define yourself by the opinion of others but by the anointing and calling God has placed on your life.

Thoughts:
_____
_____
_____
_____
_____
_____
_____

DAY 35

You can't always depend on others to lift you up and encourage you. Remember, you have the power to do it on your own. Speak well to yourself. Affirm yourself. Do it daily and watch God show up and show out in your life.

Thoughts:

_____
_____
_____
_____
_____
_____
_____

DAY 36

A person who refuses to learn is a person who will never grow.

Thoughts:

_____
_____
_____
_____
_____
_____
_____

DAY 37

Look pass cloudy moments to see the sun of hope.

Thoughts:

_____
_____
_____
_____
_____
_____
_____

DAY 38

Believing in God positions you to see the impossible become possible.

Thoughts:
_____
_____
_____
_____
_____
_____
_____

DAY 39

Prayer is never useless. It is always useful.

Thoughts:

_____
_____
_____
_____
_____
_____
_____

DAY 40

Stop and I mean stop giving other people permission to affect your happiness. If they're not happy for you, say 'see ya, don't wanna be ya.'

Thoughts:
_____
_____
_____
_____
_____
_____
_____

DAY 41

Those who are jealous and insecure of you have issues. Whatever you do, don't give in to their ignorance. It's their problem, not yours.

Thoughts:
_____
_____
_____
_____
_____
_____
_____

DAY 42

God will always humble you when you think everything is about you.

Thoughts:

DAY 43

Too much emotional baggage will wear you out and drain you. Relax. Laugh. Enjoy life. And most of all, don't trip on minor stuff.

Thoughts:

_____
_____
_____
_____
_____
_____

DAY 44

Knowing your worth keeps you from accepting things that don't add value to who you are and what you're worth.

Thoughts:
_____
_____
_____
_____
_____
_____
_____

DAY 45

A faith-flashback will cause you to remember the goodness of the Lord. In other words, when life has you down, go into your faith file to recall what God did and is able to do.

Thoughts:
_____
_____
_____
_____
_____
_____
_____

DAY 46

When what you're doing isn't getting you what you want and/or need, change you. That's right; look in the mirror and let God make you over.

Thoughts:

_____
_____
_____
_____
_____
_____
_____

DAY 47

Those who like to create drama around you are jealous of the promise and potential within you. Just know you're better than your haters.

Thoughts:
_____
_____
_____
_____
_____
_____
_____

DAY 48

No matter how messed up your life is, God can clean you up. No matter what you stand in need of, God has what you need. Just call on Him.

Thoughts:
_____
_____
_____
_____
_____
_____
_____

DAY 49

Worry weakens but faith strengthens.

Thoughts:
_____
_____
_____
_____
_____
_____
_____

DAY 50

You can't prevent others from being jealous or envious over you. Simply pray for them, continue to do what you're called to do, and allow God to deal with their insecurities.

Thoughts:
_____
_____
_____
_____
_____
_____
_____
_____

DAY 51

I don't know what you're going through or what you're dealing with, but God wanted me to deposit in your spirit that He loves you.

Thoughts:
_____
_____
_____
_____
_____
_____
_____

DAY 52

When you half-step on what you're called to do, don't expect to get positive results. Give your best if you desire to receive the best.

Thoughts:

_____
_____
_____
_____
_____
_____
_____

DAY 53

The word 'can't' keeps you in bondage, but the word 'can' frees you up. Here is another one. Fear closes the door to breakthroughs and opportunities, but faith cries out 'all things are possible for those who believe.'

Thoughts:

_____
_____
_____
_____
_____
_____
_____

DAY 54

Domestic violence is more than physical abuse. It's mental, emotional, spiritual, and cyber abuse. Don't be a victim or a perpetrator.

Thoughts:

_____
_____
_____
_____
_____
_____
_____

DAY 55

No one likes change because it moves you out of your comfort zone. When you change for the better, better blessings will come your way.

Thoughts:
___
___
___
___
___
___
___

DAY 56

When others don't support your vision, keep pressing on. God has a way of putting the right people in your life when you need it. Just be faithful to what you're called to do.

Thoughts:
_____
_____
_____
_____
_____
_____
_____

DAY 57

Your potential will attract haters and critics. Always declare to yourself, 'no weapon formed against me shall prosper.'

Thoughts:
_____
_____
_____
_____
_____
_____

DAY 58

Too many times we deal with the symptoms of a problem rather than the root cause. Once we dig below the surface and get to the root of any problem, we will begin to bring about meaningful solutions.

Thoughts:
_____
_____
_____
_____
_____
_____
_____

DAY 59

Challenge yourself daily. Without challenging yourself, you'll never discover your true potential.

Thoughts:
_____
_____
_____
_____
_____
_____
_____
_____

DAY 60

Be willing to take a stand. Be willing to step out on faith. Be willing to work for what you want. And be willing to never give up.

Thoughts:

_____
_____
_____
_____
_____
_____
_____

DAY 61

Communication is essential to a healthy relationship. When communication is done effectively, conflict and misunderstandings decrease.

Thoughts:

_____
_____
_____
_____
_____
_____
_____

DAY 62

Don't keep delaying setting goals. Begin today. No more procrastination. No more excuses. Make today count for a prosperous tomorrow.

Thoughts:
_____
_____
_____
_____
_____
_____

DAY 63

When information is shared that goes against false teachings, it's up to the recipient/student to apply what is gained. Even when it goes against popular opinion, it's still up to the recipient/student to apply the information to their life. Never stop learning.

Thoughts:

_____
_____
_____
_____
_____
_____

DAY 64

If you're unwilling to be stretched by God, then you'll never know what you're capable of doing. Trust in God. He knows what He's doing.

Thoughts:
_____
_____
_____
_____
_____
_____
_____

DAY 65

God never promised you family and/or friend support. The moment you receive a vision from the LORD, you'll face distraction from those close to you. If you are serious about doing the will of God, you will encounter spiritual warfare. Don't get discouraged. Believe in what God has called you to do.

Thoughts:

_____
_____
_____
_____
_____
_____
_____

DAY 66

Standing up for yourself will keep others from exploiting you. Even if you stand alone, I want you to understand God is with you.

Thoughts:
_____
_____
_____
_____
_____
_____
_____

DAY 67

The simplest way to deal with conflict is to keep your emotions under control.

Thoughts:
_____
_____
_____
_____
_____
_____
_____

DAY 68

People will try to get on your nerves, but you have the power to prevail. Maintain your composure and allow God to order your steps.

Thoughts:

DAY 69

No matter your past - God is able to use you to do great and marvelous things.

Thoughts:

_____
_____
_____
_____
_____
_____
_____

DAY 70

Many people have failed in life. You name it, they failed at it. However, winners use failure as a tool to get up and get ahead.

Thoughts:
_____
_____
_____
_____
_____
_____
_____

DAY 71

Faith does not depend on you rationalizing and using common sense. It's trusting in God who can make all things possible if you believe.

Thoughts:
_____
_____
_____
_____
_____
_____
_____

DAY 72

Peace begins within. That's right; when there is peace on the inside of us, then we can work on peace on the outside.

Thoughts:

_____
_____
_____
_____
_____
_____
_____

DAY 73

Those who want will 'do.' They won't complain. They won't waste their time being unproductive. They are goal-oriented and purpose-driven.

Thoughts:

_____
_____
_____
_____
_____
_____
_____

DAY 74

As a leader, you will be forced to make tough decisions. If you're afraid to do so, you won't be in business long. It's important to make sure your employees understand your vision and are working to enhance it.

Thoughts:

DAY 75

Celebrate your accomplishments. Celebrate your victories. The more you celebrate you, the more you see the wonders of God.

Thoughts:
_____
_____
_____
_____
_____
_____
_____

DAY 76

As soon as God calls you to do something, He'll begin stretching you. It's going to feel uncomfortable, but God knows what He's doing.

Thoughts:

_____
_____
_____
_____
_____
_____
_____

DAY 77

Work on your purpose in life. Even though you may get little or no support from those close to you, believe that God can work it out.

Thoughts:

_____
_____
_____
_____
_____
_____
_____

DAY 78

A poor attitude is unattractive. In fact, a poor attitude will hinder you from getting promotions, a new position, and Godly blessings.

Thoughts:

_____
_____
_____
_____
_____
_____
_____

DAY 79

Worry less and pray more. Through your prayer, you shift the focus off the problem and look towards the problem-solver.

Thoughts:
_____
_____
_____
_____
_____
_____
_____

DAY 80

Constantly seek to better yourself in all you do. You have the power to be great and do great things.

Thoughts:

DAY 81

The absence of positive reinforcement in a child's life sets them up for negative factors to infiltrate. Always find the good in a child and reinforce it constantly.

Thoughts:
___
___
___
___
___
___
___

DAY 82

Loving someone doesn't mean losing yourself. Rather it means enhancing yourself and in turn, your love will strengthen them even more.

Thoughts:

_____
_____
_____
_____
_____
_____

DAY 83

Define yourself by the Spirit of God living in you and working through you instead of what the status quo says about you.

Thoughts:
_____
_____
_____
_____
_____
_____
_____

DAY 84

Never dismiss the signs of abuse in any relationship.
You are too special to be violated.

Thoughts:
_____
_____
_____
_____
_____
_____
_____

DAY 85

Forgiveness is necessary to move pass any hurt. Without forgiving, you block blessings. Forgiveness is a process, a process that begins each day with each breath.

Thoughts:
___
___
___
___
___
___
___

DAY 86

When God graciously gives you opportunities and chances to do right and live right, you better taken them. Everyday isn't promised.

Thoughts:

DAY 87

Work done for God is never in vain. When you plant seeds into the lives of people, God does His work behind the scenes. Just be faithful.

Thoughts:
_____
_____
_____
_____
_____
_____
_____

DAY 88

Failing to value the importance of your life will keep you from enjoying life. Love your life and live it to the fullest.

Thoughts:
_____
_____
_____
_____
_____
_____
_____
_____

DAY 89

A beautiful day starts with having the right attitude. Without having the right attitude, you'll allow people and things get on your nerves. You have the power to make things happen.

Thoughts:
_____
_____
_____
_____
_____
_____
_____

DAY 90

Doubting yourself and your potential disrupts the flow of blessings coming to you. Believe in yourself and God who created you.

Thoughts:

_____
_____
_____
_____
_____
_____
_____

DAY 91

I don't care how 'fine' a person appears to be, never overlook personality, spirituality, and mentality. Inner qualities do matter.

Thoughts:
_____
_____
_____
_____
_____
_____

DAY 92

Encouraging yourself is a daily practice. The more you do it, the less likely you'll fall into the trap of depression and pity.

Thoughts:

_____
_____
_____
_____
_____
_____
_____

DAY 93

Everyday is a reason to rejoice. Always remember, it's your mentality along with your spirituality that will help enhance your reality.

Thoughts:
_____
_____
_____
_____
_____
_____
_____

DAY 94

When people try to remind you of your past mistakes, tell them you've moved on. Here's your shout - move on because God's love for you has freed you.

Thoughts:
_____
_____
_____
_____
_____
_____
_____

DAY 95

Promote peace, exhibit love, and value life. Your life matters.

Thoughts:
_____
_____
_____
_____
_____
_____
_____

DAY 96

Rebuilding your life requires you to look within yourself to make changes from the inside out.

Thoughts:
_____
_____
_____
_____
_____
_____
_____

DAY 97

Approach each day with hope, confidence, and love. Don't entertain the negative, but seek out the positive.

Thoughts:

_____
_____
_____
_____
_____
_____
_____

DAY 98

It's better to compliment than to complain. A kind word is soother than a spiteful remark. And it's much easier to love than to hate.

Thoughts:
_____
_____
_____
_____
_____
_____
_____

DAY 99

Letting go of the unproductive and unfulfilling is painful but necessary for growth. Life is too short to be held down. Here's a charge - get up and fly right.

Thoughts:
_____
_____
_____
_____
_____
_____
_____

DAY 100

Pulling life's baggage will wear you out. Allow God to handle your baggage so you can be free to receive blessings and miracles.

Thoughts:
_____
_____
_____
_____
_____
_____
_____

DAY 101

Forgiveness is a tool that brings about healing. When God forgives, He cleanses you. When you forgive, you free yourself.

Thoughts:

_____
_____
_____
_____
_____
_____
_____

DAY 102

Being addicted to alcohol, drugs, illicit sex, jealousy, envy, self-doubt, and anything ungodly destroys your spiritual temple.

Thoughts:
_____
_____
_____
_____
_____
_____
_____

DAY 103

Confident people don't brag about being confident. They simply allow their actions do all the talking for them.

Thoughts:
_____
_____
_____
_____
_____
_____

DAY 104

Throughout life, one must choose to be better, do better, and live better. It's up to you to decide when you make the step. Why not now?

Thoughts:

_____
_____
_____
_____
_____
_____
_____

DAY 105

Treat negativity like garbage - throw it out. Remember, garbage stinks and is unattractive. So is a negative attitude. Strive to be positive at all times and in all situations.

Thoughts:
___
___
___
___
___
___
___

DAY 106

Physical beauty is good but a Godly spirit is better. Working on the intangibles will make the tangibles more attractive.

Thoughts:
___

DAY 107

The ability to forgive those who hurt you is a Godly characteristic that's manifested through having a personal relationship with God.

Thoughts:
_____
_____
_____
_____
_____
_____
_____

DAY 108

You can't expect to win, if you're not willing to participate in the game. Winners don't sit on the sidelines because they refuse to lose.

Thoughts:
_____
_____
_____
_____
_____
_____
_____

DAY 109

Prayer changes things. Through prayer, you breakdown chains of insecurity and doubt and open up windows of hope, faith, and possibility.

Thoughts:

_____
_____
_____
_____
_____
_____
_____

DAY 110

No matter what you're going through, always remember that God loves you and He's forever present in your life. You are never alone.

Thoughts:

_____
_____
_____
_____
_____
_____
_____

DAY 111

When you feel good about who you are, you won't allow people and/or things define you or confine you. Feeling good internally will manifest itself outwardly.

Thoughts:
_____
_____
_____
_____
_____
_____
_____

DAY 112

When you decide in your head that you're not going to allow people or things to disrupt, interfere, or hinder your peace, you're making a conscious decision to take control over your life.

Thoughts:

_____
_____
_____
_____
_____
_____
_____

DAY 113

Refusing to grow up and mature isn't God's fault. He's done His part. Now it's up to you. When you look in the mirror and decide for better, you'll get better.

Thoughts:
_____
_____
_____
_____
_____
_____
_____

DAY 114

Jealousy and envy blind you to blessings in front of you. Be grateful for the blessings you have and watch God add and multiply.

Thoughts:
_____
_____
_____
_____
_____
_____
_____

DAY 115

When you make a mistake, don't beat yourself up. Just get up, dust yourself off, learn your lesson, and seek to do better. Forgive yourself and move on.

Thoughts:
_____
_____
_____
_____
_____
_____
_____

DAY 116

Worrying wears you out. Complaining cripples your potential. And laziness lingers your blessings. Don't give in to destructive behavior and/or actions.

Thoughts:
___
___
___
___
___
___
___

DAY 117

Jealousy and envy are thorns of ungratefulness to what God has given you. Remember to be thankful in all things. Praise God - the One who blesses.

Thoughts:
_____
_____
_____
_____
_____
_____
_____

DAY 118

It's important to understand that your life has purpose and meaning. Surround yourself with individuals who will build you up, not tear you down.

Thoughts:
___
___
___
___
___
___
___

DAY 119

Adverse moments will strengthen you to handle the blessings of tomorrow. It's through your test that you learn to lean on God's infinite wisdom.

Thoughts:

_____
_____
_____
_____
_____
_____
_____

DAY 120

Following through on the vision God has placed in your spirit will separate you from others. Stepping out on faith is about trust and the rewards are worth it.

Thoughts:

DAY 121

True love is unconditional. It doesn't have a hidden agenda nor does it focus on the material.

Thoughts:

_____
_____
_____
_____
_____
_____
_____

DAY 122

Listening to your haters is like taking sulfuric acid. It will rob you and kill you. Haters care only about destroying your dreams. Let them go NOW.

Thoughts:
_____
_____
_____
_____
_____
_____
_____

DAY 123

Never allow what others write or say about you define your worth. You're a child of God and because of your status, you can do the impossible. Believe it.

Thoughts:
_____
_____
_____
_____
_____
_____
_____

DAY 124

A grateful attitude will open up doors of possibilities that only God can open. If you find it difficult being grateful, have a faith flashback over your life.

Thoughts:
_____
_____
_____
_____
_____
_____
_____

DAY 125

A positive mindset will think positive, speak positive, and act positive. Positive people don't focus on the negative because negativity is useless and unwarranted.

Thoughts:
_____
_____
_____
_____
_____
_____
_____

DAY 126

Worrying about stuff will cause you to lose your mind and have sleepless nights. Change your outlook towards God and trust Him to handle your problem(s).

Thoughts:
_____
_____
_____
_____
_____
_____
_____

DAY 127

Erase, eradicate, and eject any negative thoughts, words, and actions from your being and see what God will do. Out with any negative and in with the positive.

Thoughts:

_____
_____
_____
_____
_____
_____
_____

DAY 128

No matter how attractive you are on the outside, using profanity robs you of the you God has called you to be. Don't allow profanity to stain your beauty.

Thoughts:

_____
_____
_____
_____
_____
_____
_____

DAY 129

Haters will always hate on you because you refuse to bow down to the spirit of settling. Don't trip on them because God has something special planned for you.

Thoughts:
_____
_____
_____
_____
_____
_____
_____

DAY 130

If you make a mistake - admit the wrong, learn the lesson, and move on. Moving pass the mistake will free you up to receive new blessings and mercies.

Thoughts:

_____
_____
_____
_____
_____
_____
_____

DAY 131

When people 'dis' and 'dismiss' you because you're doing the right thing, don't get frustrated. That means God is moving you up and clearing them out.

Thoughts:
_____
_____
_____
_____
_____
_____
_____

DAY 132

Having high expectations of yourself and for yourself isn't being arrogant. It's rising above the status quo and being the very best God has called you to be.

Thoughts:
_____
_____
_____
_____
_____
_____
_____

DAY 133

Wasting time dealing with should've, would've, and could've will deplete you of energy. Shift your focus to the 'now' so that you can have a prosperous future.

Thoughts:
_____
_____
_____
_____
_____
_____
_____

DAY 134

You deserve the best. You are strong. You can do whatever God has called you to do. Don't worry. Don't fear. And don't doubt. God's in control and has your back

Thoughts:
_____
_____
_____
_____
_____
_____
_____

DAY 135

What God has called you to do, doesn't need to be compromised because others aren't on board with you. What God has for you is for you.

Thoughts:

_____
_____
_____
_____
_____
_____
_____

DAY 136

Negativity is a virus. Get rid of it through speaking positive reinforcement into your life and distancing yourself from negative people.

Thoughts:
_____
_____
_____
_____
_____
_____
_____
_____

DAY 137

The mind is powerful weapon. With it, you can choose to win or lose, achieve or fail, break free or remain captive. Everyday decide the best for yourself.

Thoughts:
_____
_____
_____
_____
_____
_____
_____

DAY 138

Never allow the tangible of things interfere with your divine calling. Always remember- houses, cars, and money don't define you. Love you as God loves you.

Thoughts:
_____
_____
_____
_____
_____
_____
_____

DAY 139

Never apologize to others for wanting to better yourself. If they can't handle it, pray for them and move on. Use hateration as motivation for your elevation.

Thoughts:
_____
_____
_____
_____
_____
_____

DAY 140

Moving forward in life requires you to throw out those things which are weighing you down. Remember, you're too special to settle for stuff that's beneath you.

Thoughts:

_____
_____
_____
_____
_____
_____
_____

DAY 141

Unless you take the time to work on you and become the best you that you can, you won't be able to participate, elevate, and celebrate all that God has for you.

Thoughts:

___
___
___
___
___
___
___

DAY 142

When you're secure in who you are and whose you are, you don't have time to be insecure, envious, or jealous. Use your gift(s) and doors will open for you.

Thoughts:
_____
_____
_____
_____
_____
_____
_____
_____

DAY 143

When your haters place a period (.) after your life, God erases it and uses a comma (,) because He ain't through working with you, in you, and through you.

Thoughts:

_____
_____
_____
_____
_____
_____
_____

DAY 144

Kindness bestowed in the midst of chaos elevates you above the drama associated with foolishness. Define your situation and not have it define you.

Thoughts:
_____
_____
_____
_____
_____
_____
_____

DAY 145

Adversity shouldn't cause you to lose your sanity instead it should cause you to look within for strength and direction.

Thoughts:

_____
_____
_____
_____
_____
_____
_____

DAY 146

Kindness and love must be shown and displayed year round.

Thoughts:
_____
_____
_____
_____
_____
_____
_____

DAY 147

Life isn't about what you drive; it's about what's driving you.

Thoughts:

_____
_____
_____
_____
_____
_____
_____

DAY 148

Replacing fear with faith requires you to trust in God to handle all of your obstacles. Always remember, fear isn't bigger than God.

Thoughts:

_____
_____
_____
_____
_____
_____
_____

DAY 149

Stress isn't designed to kill you but to strengthen you.

Thoughts:

_____
_____
_____
_____
_____
_____
_____

DAY 150

Invest wisely and reap bountifully.

Thoughts:
_____
_____
_____
_____
_____
_____
_____

DAY 151

Whatever you're dealing with, please understand it's only temporary. Remember, 'no weapon formed against you shall prosper.'

Thoughts:
_____
_____
_____
_____
_____
_____
_____

DAY 152

Your body is a temple of God. What you put in it says a lot about how you value your temple.

Thoughts:
_____
_____
_____
_____
_____
_____
_____

DAY 153

The word 'repent' is a word often overlooked because it requires a change in one's life. Will this be the DAY you repent of things that are not Godly?

Thoughts:

_____
_____
_____
_____
_____
_____

DAY 154

Complaining about what you can't do will only delay you in accomplishing those things which you're able to do. "With Christ all things are possible."

Thoughts:

DAY 155

The word 'can't' paralyzes growth, while the word 'can' opens up opportunities that are limitless.

Thoughts:

_____
_____
_____
_____
_____
_____

DAY 156

If you want to move from being fearful to being faithful, trust in the God above you who places His Spirit in you to handle everything around you.

Thoughts:
_____
_____
_____
_____
_____
_____
_____

DAY 157

An ounce of hatred towards your fellow man is a disruptive force to the agape love God requires.

Thoughts:

_____
_____
_____
_____
_____
_____
_____

DAY 158

It's easy to praise God when things are going well, but the real character of a believer is praising Him when things are chaotic.

Thoughts:
_____
_____
_____
_____
_____
_____
_____

DAY 159

Always remember that every test will lead to your testimony. The greater your trial, the greater your blessing. Every test is temporary. Don't trip on your test, start shouting at the victory God has in store for you.

Thoughts:

_____
_____
_____
_____
_____
_____
_____

DAY 160

The true character of a person will manifest when faced with adversity.

Thoughts:
___
___
___
___
___
___
___

DAY 161

God's not finished working on you, in you, and through you.

Thoughts:
_____
_____
_____
_____
_____
_____
_____
_____

DAY 162

The best investment you could ever make in life is with God.

Thoughts:

_____
_____
_____
_____
_____
_____
_____
_____

DAY 163

Never give up on your dreams. With every breath you breath, you're one-step closer. If you can see it in your spirit than it can be manifested in the natural.

Thoughts:

_____
_____
_____
_____
_____
_____
_____

DAY 164

Your best days are ahead of you. Don't trip on the mistakes of the past. Learn from them and get ready for the blessings of the future.

Thoughts:

_____
_____
_____
_____
_____
_____
_____

DAY 165

Use every hater, rejection, and disappointment as your motivation to blow up from the floor up.

Thoughts:
_____
_____
_____
_____
_____
_____
_____

DAY 166

God opens doors to those who avail themselves to Him. Learn to trust in Him and look toward the spiritual to guide you through the natural.

Thoughts:
_____
_____
_____
_____
_____
_____
_____

DAY 167

Love those who hate on you.

Thoughts:
_____
_____
_____
_____
_____
_____
_____

DAY 168

Spiritually mature people understand who they are, why they are, and who they serve. Confusion sets in with a misplaced identity, destiny, and responsibility.

Thoughts:
_____
_____
_____
_____
_____
_____
_____
_____

DAY 169

Those committed to mediocrity will fail to step out and step forward. Why? Because true success requires having a spirit of excellence.

Thoughts:
_____
_____
_____
_____
_____
_____
_____

DAY 170

Debt is a disease that keeps one from enjoying life. Eliminate it, manage your resources, and create wealth that is generational.

Thoughts:
_____
_____
_____
_____
_____
_____
_____

DAY 171

Thoughts placed in a capsule of doubt will fail to manifest itself into an environment full of potential and possibility.

Thoughts:

_____
_____
_____
_____
_____
_____

DAY 172

Doubt is a dream killer because it seeks to cripple and paralyze your faith in the living God. In order for you to succeed in your goals and dreams, you must decide to operate under faith because faith is the prerequisite to getting blessed.

Thoughts:
_____
_____
_____
_____
_____
_____
_____

DAY 173

Conscious people are concerned about the welfare of all people, races, cultures, and ethnicities. To remain silent in the face of injustice is betrayal.

Thoughts:
___
___
___
___
___
___
___

DAY 174

Drowning yourself with guilt and disappointment prevents you from experiencing the air of blessings and deliverance.

Thoughts:
___
___
___
___
___
___
___

DAY 175

Hope is the ability to see possibility out of impossibility. A glimpse of hope has a way of providing strength to endure and carry on.

Thoughts:
_____
_____
_____
_____
_____
_____
_____

DAY 176

Opportunity doesn't prepare itself for you. You prepare for opportunity. Position yourself vertically for what God wants to do for you horizontally.

Thoughts:
_____
_____
_____
_____
_____
_____
_____

DAY 177

Fear and hope can't occupy the same space. Why? Fear is always on the defense and hope is on the offense.

Thoughts:
_____
_____
_____
_____
_____
_____
_____

DAY 178

Leaders lead with integrity whether it's in the spiritual or secular world. Church leaders should be speaking the prophetic not sleeping with the profitable. Secular leaders should be concerned with justice not political affiliation or financial kickbacks. All in all, leaders must be honest and willing to take risks to see that Right always has a seat at the table.

Thoughts:
_____
_____
_____
_____
_____
_____
_____

DAY 179

Cope with people and problems in a productive way so that you can receive a productive outcome. Proper coping techniques will save your sanity and spirit. You can overcome anything because you're a child of God.

Thoughts:
___
___
___
___
___
___
___

DAY 180

Education brings about freedom. It breaks shackles of oppression. Education liberates and transforms ones thinking. And education is a daily journey.

Thoughts:
___
___
___
___
___
___
___

DAY 181

Life has a way of enticing you with things. With the desire to obtain things, it's easy to be pulled in many directions. In all you do, seek God's guidance. You may have to say no to some things. You'll feel disappointed and may even question God in the matter. But I'm challenging you to be true to the you that God called you to be. Don't sell yourself for riches or fame.

Thoughts:
_____
_____
_____
_____
_____
_____
_____

DAY 182

Doing the right thing isn't always popular. Often times, you'll get criticized and ostracized. However, doing right keeps you faithful to your divine calling.

Thoughts:
___
___
___
___
___
___
___

DAY 183

The evils of injustice, discrimination, racism, hatred, and sexism can be overcome by love. That's right; love is a mighty cure agent.

Thoughts:
_____
_____
_____
_____
_____
_____
_____

DAY 184

True and effective leadership submits to God for guidance. Leadership isn't about being famous, instead it's about being faithful to the calling.

Thoughts:

DAY 185

How you feel about yourself internally has a way of manifesting itself externally. Simply put- always work on building yourself up and you'll see a difference.

Thoughts:
_____
_____
_____
_____
_____
_____

DAY 186

Intelligence isn't acting white instead it's being right. Success isn't for those who are lucky, but for those who put in the work. Greatness is within you.

Thoughts:
_____
_____
_____
_____
_____
_____
_____

DAY 187

Excuses keep you trapped in a box called 'defeat.' Faith, belief, persistence, and perseverance opens the door to opportunities.

Thoughts:

_____
_____
_____
_____
_____
_____
_____

DAY 188

Self-love = no abuse, no violation, no drama, nothing illegal, nothing immoral, and nothing destructive. Self-love seeks to better self through the love of God.

Thoughts:
_____
_____
_____
_____
_____
_____
_____

DAY 189

Quitting is popular for those who don't want to succeed in life. Perseverance is a lifestyle for those who wish to accomplish their goals and dreams.

Thoughts:
_____
_____
_____
_____
_____
_____

DAY 190

If you need to better yourself and/or your situation, begin today. No more waiting. No more procrastinating. The time is now. No more excuses.

Thoughts:

DAY 191

Mistakes made in your past are just that - past mistakes. Don't bring them to your present or carry them to your future. Learn from them and live better.

Thoughts:

DAY 192

The work you do today will produce a benefit tomorrow. You determine your harvest/benefit by what you plant, how you plant it, and how you nourish it.

Thoughts:
_____
_____
_____
_____
_____
_____
_____

DAY 193

When you put words into action, you'll be astonished at what you're able to accomplish. That's why it's important to speak positive.

Thoughts:

_____
_____
_____
_____
_____
_____
_____

DAY 194

Those who work through adversity will receive a great reward. On the other hand, those who quit when trouble arises will fail. Your path will have consequences.

Thoughts:
_____
_____
_____
_____
_____
_____
_____

DAY 195

Never feel the need to sacrifice your morality and/or value system to be liked. If people can't respect who you are and/or what you stand for, keep on moving.

Thoughts:
_____
_____
_____
_____
_____
_____
_____

DAY 196

Doormats are used for wiping ones feet. Never allow anyone to walk on you or over you. Your mind and spirit are powerful tools in keeping your self-worth.

Thoughts:

_____
_____
_____
_____
_____
_____
_____

DAY 197

Without acknowledging pain, there can be no healing. Pain doesn't define your worth, but it can keep you locked out of your blessings, if it's not addressed.

Thoughts:

_____
_____
_____
_____
_____
_____
_____

DAY 198

When you find your passion, you'll discover your calling. When you discover your calling, you set out on a journey to fulfill your God-given assignment.

Thoughts:
_____
_____
_____
_____
_____
_____
_____

DAY 199

Forgiving your offenders will free you up to receive blessings. When you forgive others, God will forgive you of your transgressions. Make this a forgiving day.

Thoughts:
_____
_____
_____
_____
_____
_____
_____

DAY 200

Complaining about this and complaining about that won't get you anything but frustration. Be action-oriented, do what you need to do, and make things happen.

Thoughts:
___
___
___
___
___
___
___

DAY 201

The more good you do on the outside, the more good you feed your spirit on the inside. Doing good makes you feel good, act good, and live good.

Thoughts:
___
___
___
___
___
___
___

DAY 202

Important decisions shouldn't be made in haste, but be directed through prayer. Always seek God's guidance, because His guidance is the best answer.

Thoughts:

DAY 203

A gift looses its true value while it remains in a box. Same as your gift. In order to have true value, it must be unwrapped, embraced, and used.

Thoughts:

_____
_____
_____
_____
_____
_____
_____
_____

DAY 204

Faithfulness is more than proclaiming words. It's action-oriented.

Thoughts:

_____
_____
_____
_____
_____
_____
_____

DAY 205

Giving excuses is like taking poison. It spreads throughout your body and eats away at you slowly. Avoid excuses and you'll walk into your destiny.

Thoughts:

_____
_____
_____
_____
_____
_____
_____

DAY 206

God is bigger than your problem. He's better than any circumstance/situation. And He's constantly caring for you. Hint: Turn everything over to Him.

Thoughts:
___
___
___
___
___
___
___

DAY 207

Be willing to commit yourself to thinking big and doing big. A transformed attitude will open the doors of opportunity for you to blow up from the floor up.

Thoughts:

DAY 208

Fulfilling dreams requires work. No matter how hard it seems, continue to work. Your efforts will never be in vain.

Thoughts:
_____
_____
_____
_____
_____
_____
_____

DAY 209

Set a standard of excellence for yourself in all you say and do. Always remember, half-stepping equates to receiving less than what you deserve.

Thoughts:

DAY 210

Anytime you place your life in God's hands, you're sure to get to your blessing. God hasn't forgotten you; He's just customizing your blessing.

Thoughts:
_____
_____
_____
_____
_____
_____
_____

DAY 211

In the midst of uncertainty, encourage yourself through positive affirmation. With each encouraging word you utter, you're moving out and up towards serenity.

Thoughts:

_____
_____
_____
_____
_____
_____

DAY 212

Blessings are great to receive. Thank God for the blessings. However, the blessings are never to be worshiped or idolized. God, (the Blessor) deserves worship.

Thoughts:
_____
_____
_____
_____
_____
_____
_____

DAY 213

Position yourself spiritually, mentally, and emotionally to receive your breakthrough. Submit to God, follow His Words, trust in Him, and embrace His love.

Thoughts:
_____
_____
_____
_____
_____
_____
_____

DAY 214

Trials are building blocks God uses to make you step into your purpose and blessing.

Thoughts:
_____
_____
_____
_____
_____
_____
_____
_____

DAY 215

You can't control how someone feels about you, but you can control what type of behavior and action you display towards them. Allow God's love to direct you.

Thoughts:

_____
_____
_____
_____
_____
_____

DAY 216

Your haters are always threatened by God working in you and through you. Never get discouraged or lose hope because God is setting the stage for you.

Thoughts:

DAY 217

Love is more than a feeling. It's an action that seeks the best in others no matter their past transgressions.

Thoughts:

_____
_____
_____
_____
_____
_____
_____

DAY 218

Don't shy away from life's challenges because each challenge is designed to test your faith, endurance, and character.

Thoughts:

_____
_____
_____
_____
_____
_____
_____
_____

DAY 219

Shifting your thought pattern from thinking you can to knowing you can will enable you to reach your divine destiny and be truly victorious.

Thoughts:

_____
_____
_____
_____
_____
_____
_____

DAY 220

People of strength don't need to brag about their strength, they simply exhibit it in all they say and do. Allow what's in you to do all the talking for you.

Thoughts:
_____
_____
_____
_____
_____
_____
_____

DAY 221

Today is your day to make a change. The power of God within you enables you to shed anything that's unproductive and allow you to walk in victory.

Thoughts:
_____
_____
_____
_____
_____
_____
_____

DAY 222

Showing unconditional love to your fellow neighbor means you're allowing the love of God in you to manifest itself to all around you. Love is transformational.

Thoughts:
_____
_____
_____
_____
_____
_____
_____

DAY 223

With every breath you breathe, you have the power to inhale life, possibility, and potential into your being. Don't take the air you breathe for granted.

Thoughts:
_____
_____
_____
_____
_____
_____
_____

DAY 224

If you want to be a leader, you must first learn how to follow. Those who follow with integrity are able to transition into leadership. Leadership isn't about a title; it's action-oriented that leads, guides, instructs, and builds.

Thoughts:

_____
_____
_____
_____
_____
_____
_____

DAY 225

A conceited attitude is a hindrance to what God has planned for you. Humility will open doors of prosperity and excellence.

Thoughts:
_____
_____
_____
_____
_____
_____
_____

DAY 226

Laughter is the best medicine you can have in the midst of trouble.

Thoughts:
_____
_____
_____
_____
_____
_____
_____
_____

DAY 227

Making decisions based on emotions will often times cause you to mess up and miss valuable lessons. Seek Godly wisdom and your decisions will work out fine.

Thoughts:
_____
_____
_____
_____
_____
_____
_____

DAY 228

I want you to know that you're more than a conqueror in all things. Whatever you have your mind set on, just do it. If God has spoken to you, believe it. If doubt is creeping in, rebuke it. Your life is special and you were created to do great things. Never settle for settling.

Thoughts:

_____
_____
_____
_____
_____
_____
_____

DAY 229

Walking by faith isn't about getting permission from family and friends to do God's work. It's about trusting in the One who makes all things possible.

Thoughts:

_____
_____
_____
_____
_____
_____
_____

DAY 230

Constructive criticism isn't designed to make you bitter. Instead it's used to make you better. With every constructive criticism you receive, think of it as you getting one step closer to your blessing.

Thoughts:

_____
_____
_____
_____
_____
_____
_____

DAY 231

Prosper and flourish on this day because you have what it takes to do it. Don't waste time on foolishness because foolishness won't profit you anything.

Thoughts:
_____
_____
_____
_____
_____
_____

DAY 232

Lowering your standards, values, ethics, and morality to attract and/or please others isn't Godly but foolish. Be strong in all things and trust in God.

Thoughts:
_____
_____
_____
_____
_____
_____
_____

DAY 233

It's never too late to transform your life. Why not start today? What's preventing you from beginning right now? No more excuses or procrastination. Start now.

Thoughts:

_____
_____
_____
_____
_____
_____
_____

DAY 234

When you exhibit kindness in the face of confusion, it frustrates those who are trying to hinder your progress.

Thoughts:
_____
_____
_____
_____
_____
_____
_____

DAY 235

When you love You on the inside, it manifests itself on the outside. People are attracted to individuals who exhibit confidence, assurance, and decisiveness.

Thoughts:

_____
_____
_____
_____
_____
_____
_____

DAY 236

Each day is full of what you make it. It can be joyous or disastrous. The key is allowing God to order your steps and submitting to His will for your life.

Thoughts:
_____
_____
_____
_____
_____
_____
_____

DAY 237

When people take your kindness for granted, always remember God has a way of rewarding you for doing the right thing. When people hate, God will congratulate.

Thoughts:

_____
_____
_____
_____
_____
_____
_____

DAY 238

Relationships built on taking and not on giving will fail. Every relationship must be cultivated and nourished in love with the hope of building and empowering.

Thoughts:

DAY 239

Investing in yourself today will give you a great return on your investment. With every investment, you should expect a gain in every area of your life.

Thoughts:

DAY 240

Making friends with haters, complainers, and unproductive people will ruin your chances of blowing up. Learn to distance yourself from them and live your life.

Thoughts:
_____
_____
_____
_____
_____
_____
_____

DAY 241

Sometimes you have to go through some pain in order to get your breakthrough. Pain is only temporary. God's love for you is permanent and always abundant.

Thoughts:
_____
_____
_____
_____
_____
_____
_____

DAY 242

Lazy people are a cancer to your progress. They'll try to spread their illness on you. Don't allow it to happen because a productive person receives blessings.

Thoughts:
_____
_____
_____
_____
_____
_____
_____

DAY 243

Grace and mercy are able to keep you in the protective arms of God. Your life is precious to Him and because of that, you're assured of His unconditional love.

Thoughts:
_____
_____
_____
_____
_____
_____
_____
_____

DAY 244

Average people are content with the way things are. Extraordinary people seek to excel in all things. And those who don't care, shouldn't expect anything.

Thoughts:

DAY 245

When you hate your fellow neighbor, you fail to exhibit the God in you. True love sees beyond the wrong and searches for the right. Love changes lives.

Thoughts:
_____
_____
_____
_____
_____
_____
_____

DAY 246

Coward people can't expect to receive blessings, but faithful people will receive much because they trust in God.

Thoughts:
_____
_____
_____
_____
_____
_____
_____

DAY 247

Staying in shape spiritually will prevent you from slipping into the schemes of the enemy. Spiritual preparation makes room for spiritual elevation.

Thoughts:
_____
_____
_____
_____
_____
_____

DAY 248

Happiness is attained from within. Outward factors have a way of influencing one's behavior, but in reality, you are the captain of your emotional being.

Thoughts:

_____
_____
_____
_____
_____
_____
_____

DAY 249

Freeing yourself from hypocrisy means recognizing truth, confessing truth, and living the truth. You can't be free until truth is manifested in all things.

Thoughts:
_____
_____
_____
_____
_____
_____
_____

DAY 250

When others try to limit you, the worse thing you can do is satisfy their wishes. Tap into your inner power and trust in God, knowing you can do all things.

Thoughts:

_____
_____
_____
_____
_____
_____
_____

DAY 251

Prayer is a tool by which a person can communicate their intimate feelings to God. With prayer, you'll get relief, refreshment, and answers to your questions.

Thoughts:

_____
_____
_____
_____
_____
_____
_____

DAY 252

If you want to be a Champion in life, you must get up after every knock down, and pick yourself up

Thoughts:
_____
_____
_____
_____
_____
_____
_____
_____

DAY 253

Those who remain in a state of doubt will constantly miss their blessings. Strengthen your faith and you'll see the marvelous works of the Lord.

Thoughts:

_____
_____
_____
_____
_____
_____
_____

DAY 254

The right inspiration will cause you to develop the right determination to reach your destination. Simply put - proper motivation will give you elevation.

Thoughts:
_____
_____
_____
_____
_____
_____
_____

DAY 255

It's never too late to live out your dreams. Don't allow age, money, time, people, or anything to mess with your divine purpose. With God, you can do it.

Thoughts:
_____
_____
_____
_____
_____
_____
_____

DAY 256

Patience and endurance separates you from those who won't succeed. Through every obstacle, you'll gain strength and the determination to make it.

Thoughts:
_____
_____
_____
_____
_____
_____
_____

DAY 257

Faithfulness in the face of obscurity will cause you to overcome any negative situation. It's through your faith that you can shout the victory song.

Thoughts:
_____
_____
_____
_____
_____
_____
_____

DAY 258

You can't advance in life by hanging around people who aren't about anything. When you know your purpose, you make it a point to hang around the right people.

Thoughts:
_____
_____
_____
_____
_____
_____
_____

DAY 259

While hateration isn't pleasant to receive from people, I urge you to use it as motivation to reach your destination because God will give you the elevation.

Thoughts:

_____
_____
_____
_____
_____
_____

DAY 260

When you have God ordering your steps, you don't have to doubt, be scared, or worry. God is your Comforter, Provider, and Protector.

Thoughts:

DAY 261

Shouting the word 'peace' in the midst of any storm is powerful. With your shout, you're demanding that trouble stops. Peace brings about calmness and clarity.

Thoughts:

_____
_____
_____
_____
_____
_____

DAY 262

Any relationship not based on a Godly foundation will crumble. Looks won't make it work. Personality may do for a while but a spiritual connection works.

Thoughts:

DAY 263

Failure isn't an option. Quitting isn't a vocabulary word in success. Can't is a handicap. And won't is a paralysis. Believe in yourself in all you do.

Thoughts:
___
___
___
___
___
___
___

DAY 264

Staying in your comfort zone may appear good, but in reality, you're cheating yourself out of the many blessings that's laid up for you. (Think about it)

Thoughts:

DAY 265

Complaining about the lack of opportunities won't get you anywhere in life. In order to succeed, you must be determined, motivated, and committed to excel.

Thoughts:

_____
_____
_____
_____
_____
_____
_____

DAY 266

Those who are humbled and sincere in their ways will receive blessings from the Lord. However, those who are arrogant and cocky will be disappointed.

Thoughts:

DAY 267

Quiet moments of meditation will help you gain a better perspective of your divine calling. Through being silent, God will speak to you in His clear voice.

Thoughts:
_____
_____
_____
_____
_____
_____

DAY 268

When you're focused and committed to excellence, you're not acting cocky, rather you're displaying a level of determination to reach your destination.

Thoughts:

DAY 269

Always keep your head up no matter what you're going through. Life has its problems but at the end of every problem is a rainbow full of hope and possibility.

Thoughts:

_____
_____
_____
_____
_____
_____
_____

DAY 270

Honesty and integrity are traits that will separate you from the crowd. When you have the right attitude, God will take you to the right altitude.

Thoughts:
___
___
___
___
___
___
___

DAY 271

When you think you can't, God steps in and says you can.

Thoughts:

_____
_____
_____
_____
_____
_____
_____

DAY 272

The truth sets you free from bondage. It allows you to move pass lies, deception, and darkness. That's right; the truth enables you to see the light.

Thoughts:
_____
_____
_____
_____
_____
_____
_____

DAY 273

Never take the One you love and who loves you for granted. If so, you'll find yourself messed up. Never take your eyes off God in whatever you do.

Thoughts:
_____
_____
_____
_____
_____
_____
_____

DAY 274

Temporary setbacks will lead to blessings on the other side. Setbacks are designed to make you better, not bitter. Be better than your setback.

Thoughts:
_____
_____
_____
_____
_____
_____
_____

DAY 275

Opportunities are available to those who position themselves to succeed. Without positioning yourself mentally, physically, and spiritually, you'll be left out.

Thoughts:
_____
_____
_____
_____
_____
_____

DAY 276

God will take care of you. He will never leave you nor forsake you. He does provide chances for you to get your life right. Keep your faith in Him always.

Thoughts:
_____
_____
_____
_____
_____
_____
_____

DAY 277

Getting ahead in life means disregarding that which is negative and detrimental to your growth and embracing all that is positive, productive, and fruitful.

Thoughts:

_____
_____
_____
_____
_____
_____
_____

DAY 278

Every problem has a solution attached to it. The key is working toward the solution and not getting caught up in the problem.

Thoughts:
_____
_____
_____
_____
_____
_____
_____

DAY 279

When you find yourself in a jam, don't trip out or freak out. Seek divine guidance, allow God to order your steps, and submit to His loving will.

Thoughts:

_____
_____
_____
_____
_____
_____
_____

DAY 280

Don't expect others to love you, respect you, and treat you well, if you don't do it for yourself. Set the standard for yourself and others will follow.

Thoughts:

_____
_____
_____
_____
_____
_____
_____

DAY 281

Feeling good about yourself will elevate yourself above normality into a state of knowing that you can do all things and never fail.

Thoughts:
___
___
___
___
___
___
___

DAY 282

When you allow your spirituality to take over your mentality, you begin to shape a productive reality.

Thoughts:
_____
_____
_____
_____
_____
_____
_____

DAY 283

Challenge yourself to rise above the stereotypes people place on you. Use the ignorance of others of you and about you to show them you can succeed.

Thoughts:

_____
_____
_____
_____
_____
_____
_____

DAY 284

God specializes in taking what others claim as impossible and making it a reality. Here's your assignment - live out your dreams and reach for the moon.

Thoughts:
_____
_____
_____
_____
_____
_____
_____

DAY 285

The words you speak out of your mouth can either build up or tear down. Remember, what you speak comes from the heart.

Thoughts:

DAY 286

Refuse to hang with negative people because they will drain and deplete you. Associate with positive and productive people who will fill you with energy and hope.

Thoughts:

_____
_____
_____
_____
_____
_____
_____

DAY 287

To get ahead in life, you must have the following: faith, self-determination, persistence, belief, discipline, and vision. With these, you're bound to achieve.

Thoughts:

_____
_____
_____
_____
_____
_____
_____

DAY 288

Never limit yourself due to your surroundings. In other words, see yourself as a superstar worthy of doing and achieving great things. It's in you to succeed.

Thoughts:
_____
_____
_____
_____
_____
_____
_____

DAY 289

Carrying unnecessary baggage in life will weigh you down and slow you down from reaching your destination. Dump that baggage and travel light.

Thoughts:

_____
_____
_____
_____
_____
_____
_____

DAY 290

Hold yourself responsible and accountable for your actions. Never give people permission to control you. If you do, you'll miss all that God has for you

Thoughts:
_____
_____
_____
_____
_____
_____
_____

DAY 291

If God has compelled you to do something, what are you waiting on? Trust in Him, step out on faith, believe that He's called you, and watch what happens.

Thoughts:
___
___
___
___
___
___
___

DAY 292

If you fall down while striving to reach your goal, don't get discouraged; just get up because God has a way of turning disappointments into divine blessings.

Thoughts:
_____
_____
_____
_____
_____
_____
_____

DAY 293

God specializes in transforming lives from the inside out. In other words, no matter what you're dealing with or going through, God is able to work it out.

Thoughts:

_____
_____
_____
_____
_____
_____
_____

DAY 294

When others try to discredit you because of your spiritual gift, don't get angry or frustrated. Say 'take it up with God', the One who gives and blesses.

Thoughts:
_____
_____
_____
_____
_____
_____
_____

DAY 295

Leaders are people of influence, not dictators or agitators. To lead, you must have a vision, communicate it, and associate with like-minded people.

Thoughts:
_____
_____
_____
_____
_____
_____

DAY 296

You're not called to live less than your potential because you're hooked up with God. With your divine hookup, you're able to walk in victory.

Thoughts:
_____
_____
_____
_____
_____
_____
_____

DAY 297

Following your dreams means staying on the course in which God has directed you. Don't stray because of haters. Just keep your eyes on the ultimate prize.

Thoughts:
_____
_____
_____
_____
_____
_____
_____

DAY 298

Goodness and mercy are the twin attributes of God which enables you to face any situation and know beyond any shadow of doubt, you have the victory.

Thoughts:

_____
_____
_____
_____
_____
_____
_____

DAY 299

Disciplining yourself to make changes for the best requires work. It's more than talk; it's about consciously deciding you have the power to make things happen.

Thoughts:
_____
_____
_____
_____
_____
_____
_____

DAY 300

Smiling in the midst of pain and uncertainty causes the enemy to be confused. Why? Through your smile, you're proclaiming you have inner power that guides you.

Thoughts:

_____
_____
_____
_____
_____
_____
_____

DAY 301

Love yourself so much that you never lose the you that God created you to be. You are special, talented, and gifted.

Thoughts:
_____
_____
_____
_____
_____
_____

DAY 302

What's stopping you from doing what you want to do? Fear? Doubt? Confusion? Remember, if God called you, He'll make a way for you to succeed and prosper.

Thoughts:
_____
_____
_____
_____
_____
_____
_____

DAY 303

No matter what you're going through on the outside, never allow it to affect how you feel about yourself on the inside. You are a person of value and worth.

Thoughts:
_____
_____
_____
_____
_____
_____
_____

DAY 304

Learn from your mistakes by being teachable, disciplined, and determined to correct what's wrong so that you can be the best you that God has called you to be.

Thoughts:

_____
_____
_____
_____
_____
_____
_____

DAY 305

Being educated isn't being nerdy. It's through being educated that you create opportunities, reach higher heights, and seek all that God has for you.

Thoughts:
_____
_____
_____
_____
_____
_____
_____

DAY 306

Obstacles are not designed for you to quit. They are designed to make you persevere and press on to your goal. Every obstacle has a blessing on the other side.

Thoughts:
_____
_____
_____
_____
_____
_____
_____

DAY 307

A transformed mind is able to rise above the status quo. A transformed heart is able to love when there is hatred all around. A transformed person is powerful.

Thoughts:

DAY 308

The best way to move pass any disappointment is to funeralize it, bury it, and get on with your life. Life does continue after disappointments.

Thoughts:
_____
_____
_____
_____
_____
_____
_____

DAY 309

Without a willingness to better yourself, you can't expect to receive the best. Strive to be the best in all things and refuse to be average.

Thoughts:
___
___
___
___
___
___
___

DAY 310

Faith is able to carry you over hurdles, get you through difficulties, and cause you to reach your divine destiny. Faith, don't leave home without it.

Thoughts:
___
___
___
___
___
___
___

DAY 311

Persist in the midst of opposition. When difficulties and doubt rise up against you, keep your head up, stay focused, and trust in the Lord.

Thoughts:

_____
_____
_____
_____
_____
_____
_____

DAY 312

Your voice counts. Your opinion matters. Never remain silent in the face of injustice because you have a responsibility in this life. Don't settle for defeat.

Thoughts:

DAY 313

Growing pains are never pleasant, however, the pain of growing up is necessary for great things to happen. Your growing pain is a prerequisite to your blessing.

Thoughts:
_____
_____
_____
_____
_____
_____

DAY 314

Good and mediocre traveled on a road together. When trouble came, mediocre stopped and complained, but good looked within itself and pressed on.

Thoughts:
___
___
___
___
___
___
___

DAY 315

Disappointments are never designed to devalue your worth but to move you one step closer to your blessing/breakthrough.

Thoughts:
___
___
___
___
___
___
___

DAY 316

Maximize opportunity. Minimize waste. Elevate your consciousness. Decease lack of knowledge. Strive to be #1. Refuse to settle for less.

Thoughts:

DAY 317

The value you place on yourself and your time will enable you to be more productive and less wasteful. Always remember, you are an asset not a liability.

Thoughts:
_____
_____
_____
_____
_____
_____
_____

DAY 318

Conquering the obstacles of life requires patience, persistence, determination, and commitment. Never give up, never give in, and stay focused.

Thoughts:
_____
_____
_____
_____
_____
_____
_____

DAY 319

The impression you make on others will either open or close doors. Project an image of confidence and assurance and you'll get noticed and elevated.

Thoughts:

_____
_____
_____
_____
_____
_____

DAY 320

Set high expectations for yourself and believe that all things are possible. Refuse to settle for settling and never give in to mediocrity.

Thoughts:
___
___
___
___
___
___
___

DAY 321

Adversity is designed to make you better not bitter.
With every obstacle you encounter, you'll discover
God's strength inside of you to press on.

Thoughts:

_____
_____
_____
_____
_____
_____
_____

DAY 322

Wisdom keeps you on the right path. Foolishness will keep you in the dark. Seek knowledge, search for wisdom, apply what you learn, and live victoriously.

Thoughts:
___
___
___
___
___
___
___

DAY 323

Procrastinating on what you need to do will delay what God has for you. Those who want and need God to move will act with a sense of urgency and get blessed.

Thoughts:

_____
_____
_____
_____
_____
_____
_____

DAY 324

Giving up forfeits your right to success. Only those who are committed, passionate, and determined will taste and see that success is good.

Thoughts:
_____
_____
_____
_____
_____
_____
_____

DAY 325

You are creatively designed to break down barriers. How so? Because the Spirit of God dwelling in you is greater than any 'hell' outside of you.

Thoughts:

_____
_____
_____
_____
_____
_____

DAY 326

Faith unlocks the door to opportunities. Fear keeps the door shut. Faith gives you unexpected blessings. Fear prevents you from receiving.

Thoughts:
___
___
___
___
___
___
___

DAY 327

Distancing yourself from success will always keep you in the rear room looking, wanting, hoping, and wishing. Only those who want success can receive it.

Thoughts:
_____
_____
_____
_____
_____
_____
_____

DAY 328

With each step you take in your journey, make positive and productive choices. Learn what you can so that you can be all that God has called you to be.

Thoughts:
_____
_____
_____
_____
_____
_____
_____

DAY 329

Breaking the yoke(s) of complacency that keeps you in bondage will open doors for you to blow up from the floor up.

Thoughts:
_____
_____
_____
_____
_____
_____
_____
_____

DAY 330

When you remove yourself from your problems and allow God to intervene, then you're able to look ahead to the blessings He has for you.

Thoughts:
_____
_____
_____
_____
_____
_____
_____

DAY 331

Change is necessary when you decide to do better.
Without change, you'll remain stuck and tied up.
Change frees you up to receive what God has for you.

Thoughts:

_____
_____
_____
_____
_____
_____
_____

DAY 332

Define yourself by the God above you who lives within you and is able to guide you.

Thoughts:
_____
_____
_____
_____
_____
_____
_____

DAY 333

Kind words spoken in troubling times can elevate a person from being sad to being hopeful. The power of words are able to build up and cause miracles.

Thoughts:

_____
_____
_____
_____
_____
_____
_____

DAY 334

Failing to better yourself will keep you crippled and paralyzed in a state of settling. Expect the best and you'll keep moving forward to greatness.

Thoughts:

DAY 335

Winners know how to operate with success. They are grateful, appreciative, and thankful. When they win, they walk with confidence. No exaggeration needed.

Thoughts:

DAY 336

Determined and passionate people are bound to succeed in life. On the other hand, lazy people will miss their blessings and complain. Be a winner today.

Thoughts:

DAY 337

Without reading, questioning, analyzing, and challenging what you hear on the news, you'll be misled. Educate yourself so that no one can steer you wrong.

Thoughts:

_____
_____
_____
_____
_____
_____

DAY 338

Healthy living means depositing the right things in your body and surrounding yourself around positive people. You get out what you put it.

Thoughts:
_____
_____
_____
_____
_____
_____
_____

DAY 339

When addressing difficult situations, remain calm, respectful, open-minded, peaceful, and prayed-up. In all things, allow God to order your steps.

Thoughts:

_____
_____
_____
_____
_____
_____

DAY 340

Never make an excuse for not trying.

Thoughts:
_____
_____
_____
_____
_____
_____
_____

DAY 341

Forsake all that is harmful to the building up of your spiritual temple. Never say what's impossible because God has given you the power to overcome all things.

Thoughts:
_____
_____
_____
_____
_____
_____
_____

DAY 342

High expectations mean you want much. Low expectations mean you'll settle for simply anything. No expectation means you don't want anything.

Thoughts:
_____
_____
_____
_____
_____
_____
_____

DAY 343

I challenge you to not allow fear to determine your destiny. God's vision and calling on your life should not be stifled. Operate in faith and watch God move.

Thoughts:

DAY 344

Planning your day in advance will keep you focused on your goals and eliminate unnecessary distractions. If you don't make a plan, confusion is inevitable.

Thoughts:
_____
_____
_____
_____
_____
_____
_____

DAY 345

Doing great things isn't about people-pleasing, rather it's allowing the divine nature of God work in you and through you to make a difference.

Thoughts:

_____
_____
_____
_____
_____
_____
_____

DAY 346

Optimism in the face of adversity will develop character to succeed.

Thoughts:
_____
_____
_____
_____
_____
_____
_____

DAY 347

Seek to grow in every area of your life. Don't just talk about it, simply do it. Don't allow procrastination and/or fear stop you from achieving your goals.

Thoughts:
_____
_____
_____
_____
_____
_____
_____

DAY 348

Sickness and illness don't have the final answer over your life. Use the temporary down- time as time spent with God listening to what He has to say to you.

Thoughts:
_____
_____
_____
_____
_____
_____
_____

DAY 349

What seems like common sense to you may not be common sense to others. Effective communication between everyone will alleviate problems, challenges and issues.

Thoughts:
_____
_____
_____
_____
_____
_____
_____

DAY 350

Issues left undone now will become huge obstacles tomorrow. Work hard to correct what's happening now so you won't have to deal with the headaches later.

Thoughts:
_____
_____
_____
_____
_____
_____
_____

DAY 351

Time is precious. You can either use it wisely or waste it foolishly. Always remember, success is rewarded through time management. Make time work for you.

Thoughts:
___
___
___
___
___
___
___

DAY 352

Training to be the best requires work, sacrifice, commitment, passion, and dedication. What you put in will determine how much or how little you get in return.

Thoughts:
_____
_____
_____
_____
_____
_____
_____

DAY 353

When we see man as neither inferior nor superior to any race, gender, or ethnicity, then the chains of prejudice, racism, and disharmony will be destroyed.

Thoughts:
_____
_____
_____
_____
_____
_____
_____

DAY 354

Blaming others for your shortcomings will keep you caged in. Here's a challenge: Rise above their injustice and hatred and allow God to order your steps.

Thoughts:

DAY 355

Mediocrity and excellence tried hanging out one day but decided it wasn't feasible. Mediocrity likes being average, but excellence wants the best in everything.

Thoughts:

DAY 356

When you have 'bounce-back' ability, you come to realize when people try to knock you down, the more you're able to 'bounce-back' stronger and more committed.

Thoughts:

DAY 357

Live with purpose and meaning. Never surrender what God has called you to do for anything. Your life is valuable and with that, you can reach your goal(s).

Thoughts:

DAY 358

Your dream(s) should never be deferred because dreams provide insight into what God has planned for you.

Thoughts:
___
___
___
___
___
___
___

DAY 359

It's one thing knowing people in places for a hook-up, but the real hook-up is having a relationship with God. Remember - God can do what no one else can.

Thoughts:

DAY 360

Never leave your faith at the door when you work, go to school, or hang out. Nothing and no one should separate you from the love of God.

Thoughts:
_____
_____
_____
_____
_____
_____
_____

DAY 361

Monitor yourself daily to make sure you're being true to the you God has called you to be. Daily check-ups will do the mind, body, and soul good.

Thoughts:

_____
_____
_____
_____
_____
_____
_____

DAY 362

With each step you take, you determine your direction. Step forward - get what God has for you. Step backward - get nowhere. It's up to you.

Thoughts:
_____
_____
_____
_____
_____
_____
_____

DAY 363

Breaking free of the hateration in your life is more than physical separation. It's breaking free mentally, psychologically, and emotionally of all negativity.

Thoughts:
_____
_____
_____
_____
_____
_____
_____

DAY 364

When the world treats you as an 'underdog,' God treats you as the Victor. With God working in you and through you, you can claim the victory.

Thoughts:
_____
_____
_____
_____
_____
_____
_____
_____

DAY 365

When you demand the best from yourself in all that you set out to do, it will transfer to demanding that others give their best. No half-steppin allowed.

Thoughts:
___
___
___
___
___
___
___

Made in United States
Troutdale, OR
08/09/2024

21874323R10206